MACHINES CLOSE-UP

MODERN MILITARY AIRCRAFT

Daniel Gilpin and Alex Pang

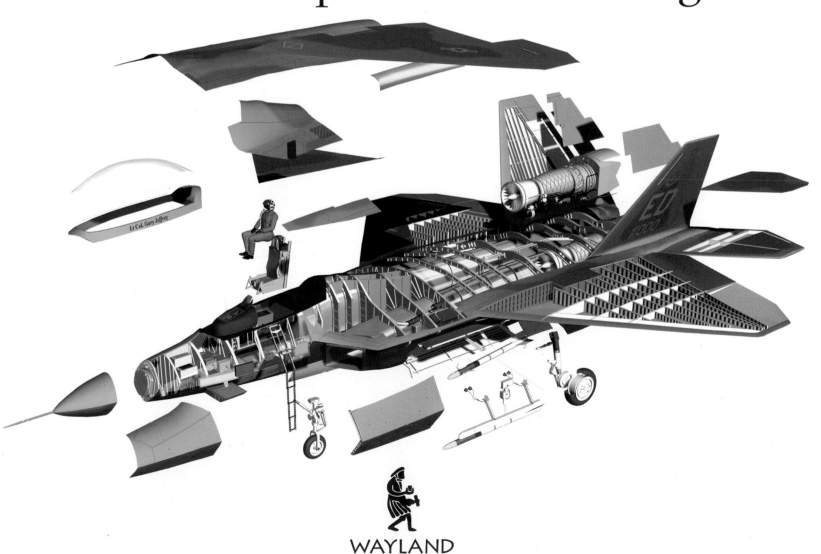

WAYLAND

This edition published in 2009 by Wayland

Wayland
Hachette Children's Books
338 Euston Road
London NW1 3BH

Wayland Australia
Level 17/207 Kent Street
Sydney, NSW 2000

Produced by
David West ⚇ Children's Books
7 Princeton Court
55 Felsham Road
London SW15 1AZ

Designer: Gary Jeffrey
Illustrator: Alex Pang
Editor: Katharine Pethick
Consultant: Steve Parker

A CIP catalogue record for this book is available
from the British Library.

ISBN: 9780750260732

Printed in China

Wayland is a division of
Hachette Children's Books,
an Hachette UK company.
www.hachette.co.uk

PHOTO CREDITS :
Abbreviations: t-top, m-middle, b-bottom, r-right,
l-left, c-centre.
6r, Isabelle + Stéphane Gallay; 6l, access.denied;
6bl, 7r, U.S. Airforce; 8t, Robert Lawton; 8,
Paul Maritz; 9t, hoyasmeg; 9bl, U.S. Airforce
photo; 9br, Smudge 9000

CONTENTS

INTRODUCTION

Modern military aircraft include some of the fastest, most technologically advanced and most expensive vehicles in the world. Each one is designed and its prototype tested over a period of several years before it is produced and enters service.

GENERATIONS FLY PAST
An F-15 Eagle (bottom), F/A-22 Raptor (top), and an A-10 Thunderbolt (right) fly in formation with a US Mustang fighter plane from World War II.

F/A-22 Raptor

US Mustang

A-10 Thunderbolt

F-15 Eagle

HOW THIS BOOK WORKS

MAIN TEXT

Explains the history of the aircraft and outlines its primary role. Other information, such as which forces use the aircraft, is also covered here.

SPECS

Gives information about the aircraft's dimensions, speed and weapons carrying capacity.

INTERESTING FEATURES

This box contains a detailed illustration of the engine or another design feature that makes the aircraft unique. Informative text explains the feature's function.

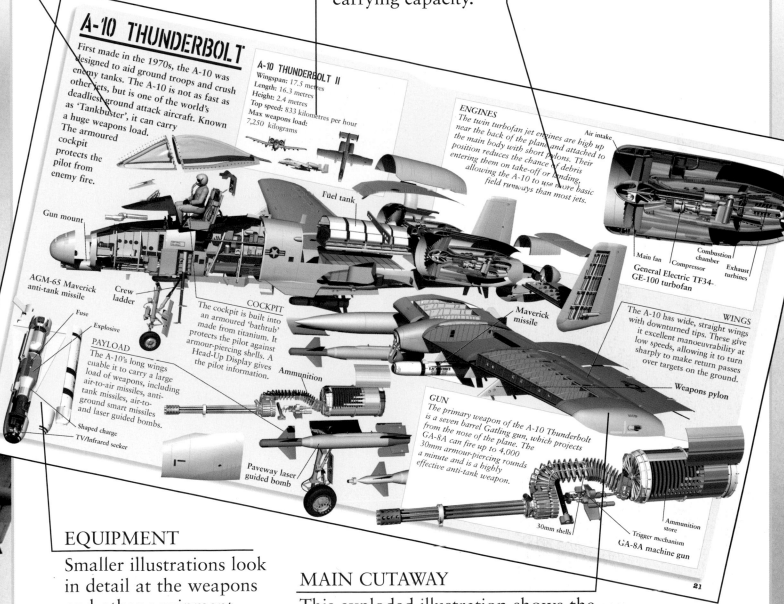

A-10 THUNDERBOLT

First made in the 1970s, the A-10 was designed to aid ground troops and crush enemy tanks. The A-10 is not as fast as other jets, but is one of the world's deadliest ground attack aircraft. Known as 'Tankbuster', it can carry a huge weapons load. The armoured cockpit protects the pilot from enemy fire.

A-10 THUNDERBOLT II
Wingspan: 17.5 metres
Length: 16.3 metres
Height: 2.4 metres
Top speed: 833 kilometres per hour
Max weapons load: 7,250 kilograms

ENGINES
The twin turbofan jet engines are high up near the back of the plane and attached to the main body with short pylons. Their position reduces the chance of debris entering them on take-off or landing, allowing the A-10 to use more basic field runways than most jets.

Air intake
Main fan
Compressor
Combustion chamber
Exhaust turbines
General Electric TF34-GE-100 turbofan

Fuel tank

Gun mount

AGM-65 Maverick anti-tank missile

Crew ladder

COCKPIT
The cockpit is built into an armoured 'bathtub' made from titanium. It protects the pilot against armour-piercing shells. A Head-Up Display gives the pilot information.

PAYLOAD
The A-10's long wings enable it to carry a large load of weapons, including air-to-air missiles, anti-tank missiles, air-to-ground smart missiles and laser guided bombs.

Fuse
Explosive
Shaped charge
TV/Infrared seeker

Maverick missile

WINGS
The A-10 has wide, straight wings with downturned tips. These give it excellent manoeuvrability at low speeds, allowing it to turn sharply to make return passes over targets on the ground.

Weapons pylon

Ammunition

GUN
The primary weapon of the A-10 Thunderbolt is a seven barrel Gatling gun, which projects from the nose of the plane. The GA-8A can fire up to 4,000 30mm armour-piercing rounds a minute and is a highly effective anti-tank weapon.

Paveway laser guided bomb

30mm shells

Ammunition store
Trigger mechanism
GA-8A machine gun

20

21

EQUIPMENT

Smaller illustrations look in detail at the weapons and other equipment carried by the aircraft to carry out different roles.

MAIN CUTAWAY

This exploded illustration shows the internal structure of the aircraft and gives information on the positions of its various working parts.

PROPS TO JETS

The earliest military aircraft were balloons, used for warfare in 1849. During World War I planes replaced balloons, primarily because they were much easier to direct and control.

FLYING CRATES

In World War I, planes were used for reconnaissance. In 1914, when battles were fought from trenches, planes could fly over and then give commanders the information they needed to target enemy positions and plan their attacks.

FOKKER DR1

BOEING P-26
Nicknamed 'the peashooter', this was the first all-metal fighter.

STREAMLINED
Early planes were built with little thought given to overall speed. Between the wars that began to change. Streamlining became an important feature of plane design. Together with improvements in engine technology, this made planes much quicker.

FOKKER EINDECKER
This 1915 fighter was the first with synchroniser gear, which controlled gunfire through the spinning propeller.

SPAD S.XIII
This French-built biplane was a very capable fighter of World War I. 8,472 were made.

HANDLEY PAGE 0/100
This World War 1 bomber was one of the largest early biplanes.

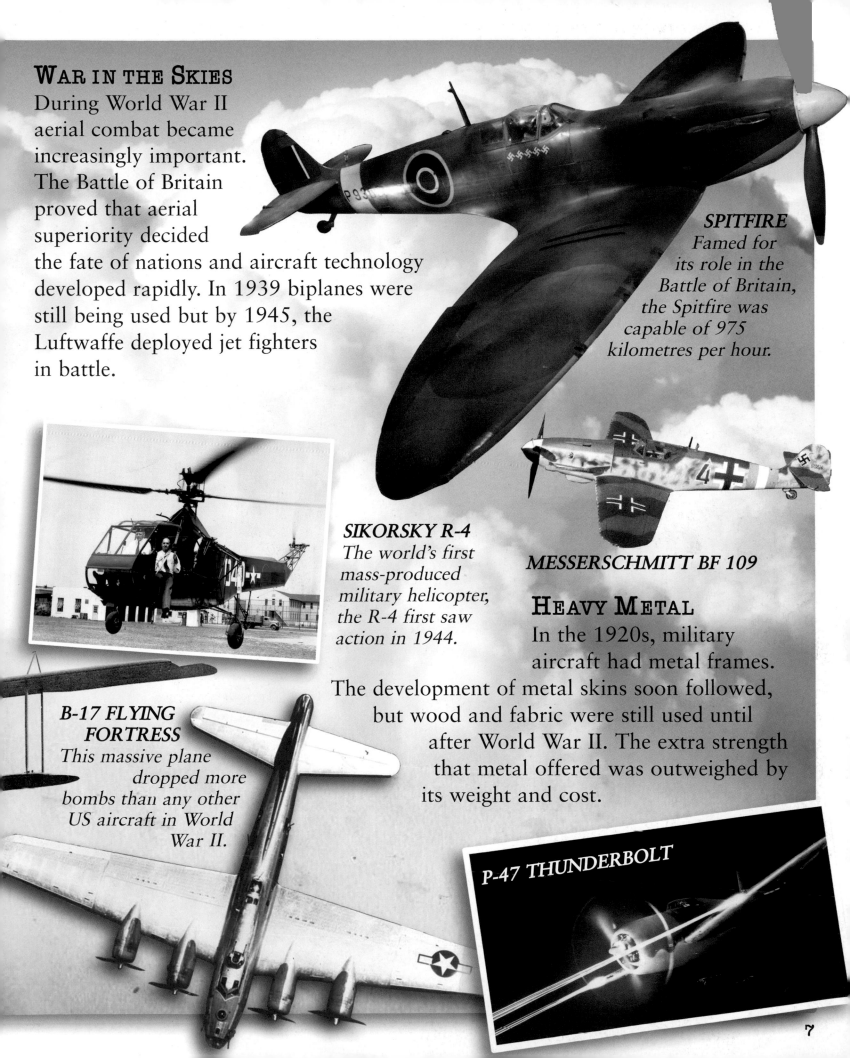

WAR IN THE SKIES

During World War II aerial combat became increasingly important. The Battle of Britain proved that aerial superiority decided the fate of nations and aircraft technology developed rapidly. In 1939 biplanes were still being used but by 1945, the Luftwaffe deployed jet fighters in battle.

SPITFIRE
Famed for its role in the Battle of Britain, the Spitfire was capable of 975 kilometres per hour.

SIKORSKY R-4
The world's first mass-produced military helicopter, the R-4 first saw action in 1944.

MESSERSCHMITT BF 109

HEAVY METAL

In the 1920s, military aircraft had metal frames. The development of metal skins soon followed, but wood and fabric were still used until after World War II. The extra strength that metal offered was outweighed by its weight and cost.

B-17 FLYING FORTRESS
This massive plane dropped more bombs than any other US aircraft in World War II.

P-47 THUNDERBOLT

THE JET AGE

The first operational jet fighter, the German Messerschmitt ME 262, appeared too late in World War II to make a big impact but it brought in a new era in military aircraft design.

WING SWEPT

The ME 262 had relatively straight wings, like propeller-driven planes. As jet fighters developed their wings became more swept back. As wing shape changed so did the position of the engines, which moved into the fuselage. Larger planes, such as bombers, kept their engines on the wings.

MIG 17
This Soviet jet of 1952 was one of the first with 'swept' wings, to reduce drag for increased speed.

F-86 SABRE
This US fighter was introduced in 1949. The last active units were retired by the Bolivian Air Force in 1994.

LIGHTNING F.3
This 1959 British jet fighter was the first plane capable of cruising at more than the speed of sound without afterburners.

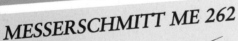

MESSERSCHMITT ME 262

PUSHING THE ENVELOPE

The incredible power of the jet engine encouraged experiments with design. Developed for speed in 1947, the YB-49 Flying Wing bomber was ahead of its time. However, due to severe design limitations, especially when bombing, it remained a prototype.

YB-49 FLYING WING

WHIRLYBIRDS

As jets started to replace propellers in planes, another group of aircraft began to appear on military airfields – the helicopters. Like jet fighters, the first military helicopters went into action near the end of World War II. Since then they have had a vital role in most air forces.

BELL XV-3
The first successful tiltrotor aircraft, it inspired today's V-22 Osprey.

HUEY COBRA
First flown in 1965, the Huey remains in active service with several air forces around the world.

F-117 STEALTH FIGHTER

SUKHOI SU-30

TOP GUNS

Today's modern jets are the result of more than a century of military aviation history. Some jets can travel at more than twice the speed of sound. Others are all but invisible to radar. Their pilots face danger but surely have one of the best jobs in the world.

F/A-22 RAPTOR
The F/A-22 Raptor is state-of-the-art, combining high speed with stealth technology.

EUROFIGHTER TYPHOON
Introduced in 2003, this plane is in service with the Royal Air Force, Luftwaffe and Italian and Spanish Air Forces.

AH-64 LONGBOW APACHE

The AH-64 is the world's most advanced armed helicopter in active service. Designed in 1981, it destroys hard targets such as tanks. The cockpit and fuel tanks are heavily armoured, withstanding hits from rounds up to 23mm.

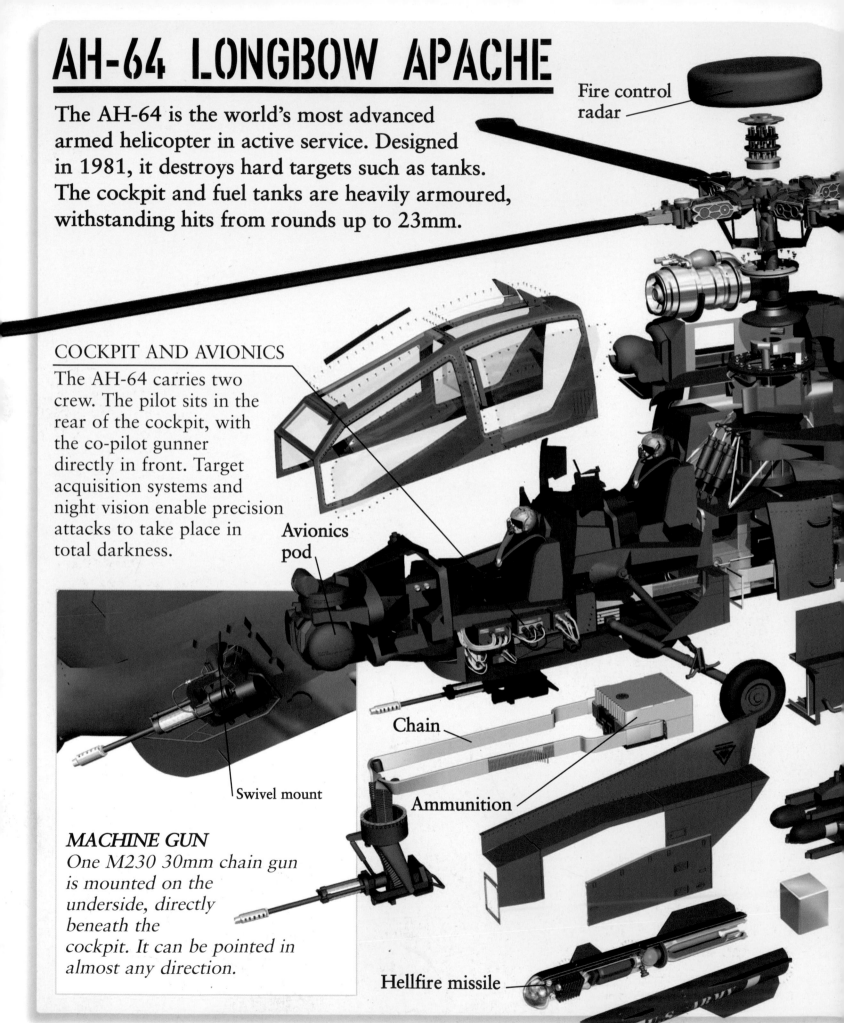

Fire control radar

COCKPIT AND AVIONICS

The AH-64 carries two crew. The pilot sits in the rear of the cockpit, with the co-pilot gunner directly in front. Target acquisition systems and night vision enable precision attacks to take place in total darkness.

Avionics pod

Swivel mount

Chain

Ammunition

MACHINE GUN

One M230 30mm chain gun is mounted on the underside, directly beneath the cockpit. It can be pointed in almost any direction.

Hellfire missile

AH-64 LONGBOW APACHE

Rotor diameter: 14.6 metres
Length: 17.7 metres
Height: 4.6 metres
Top speed: 293 kilometres per hour
Max weapons load: 1,900 kilograms

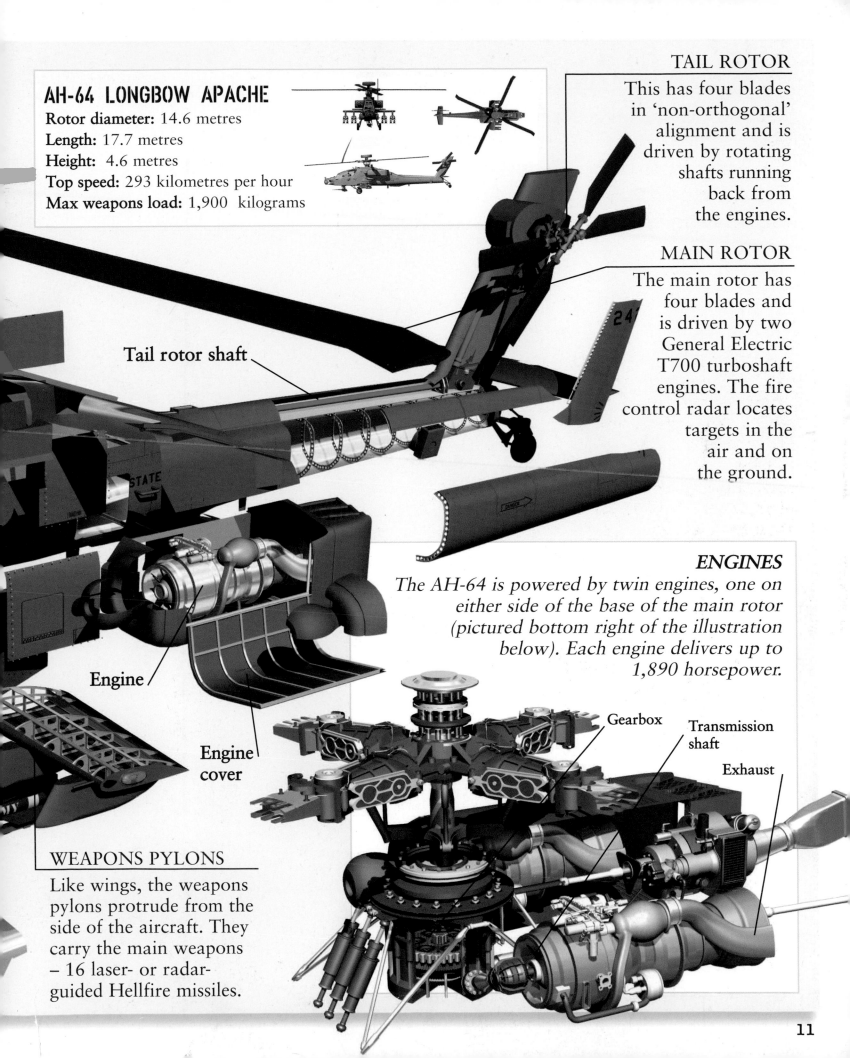

TAIL ROTOR

This has four blades in 'non-orthogonal' alignment and is driven by rotating shafts running back from the engines.

MAIN ROTOR

The main rotor has four blades and is driven by two General Electric T700 turboshaft engines. The fire control radar locates targets in the air and on the ground.

Tail rotor shaft

ENGINES

The AH-64 is powered by twin engines, one on either side of the base of the main rotor (pictured bottom right of the illustration below). Each engine delivers up to 1,890 horsepower.

Engine

Engine cover

Gearbox

Transmission shaft

Exhaust

WEAPONS PYLONS

Like wings, the weapons pylons protrude from the side of the aircraft. They carry the main weapons – 16 laser- or radar-guided Hellfire missiles.

F-35 LIGHTNING II

Formerly known as the JSF, or Joint Strike Fighter, the F-35 Lightning II was commissioned by the US Army from Lockheed Martin to replace the F-16, A-10, F/A-18 and AV-8B fleet of tactical fighter aircraft. The first test versions of the F-35 flew in 2006, followed by about five years of development time before going into active service.

F-35 LIGHTNING II

Wingspan: 10.7 metres
Length: 15.4 metres
Height: 5.3 metres
Top speed: 1,931 kilometres per hour
Max weapons load: 8,170 kilograms

COCKPIT

The pilot flies using a right-hand side-stick and a left-hand throttle, and sits on a Martin-Baker US16E ejection seat.

GLIDE BOMB

The F-35 Lightning II can carry a range of weapons. One of these is the AGM-154 glide bomb. It has a range of 130 kilometres, so can be launched at a safe distance from the enemy. It uses GPS to guide it towards its target.

Helmet screen display system

Cockpit display

Guidance systems

Explosive payload

AGM-154 glide bomb

Nose spike

Lift fan

SENSORS

The plane's radar system is mounted inside its nose. Underneath the nose cone is an electro-optical targeting system.

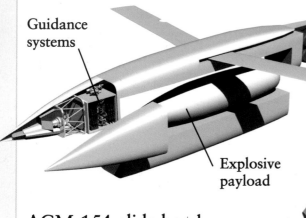

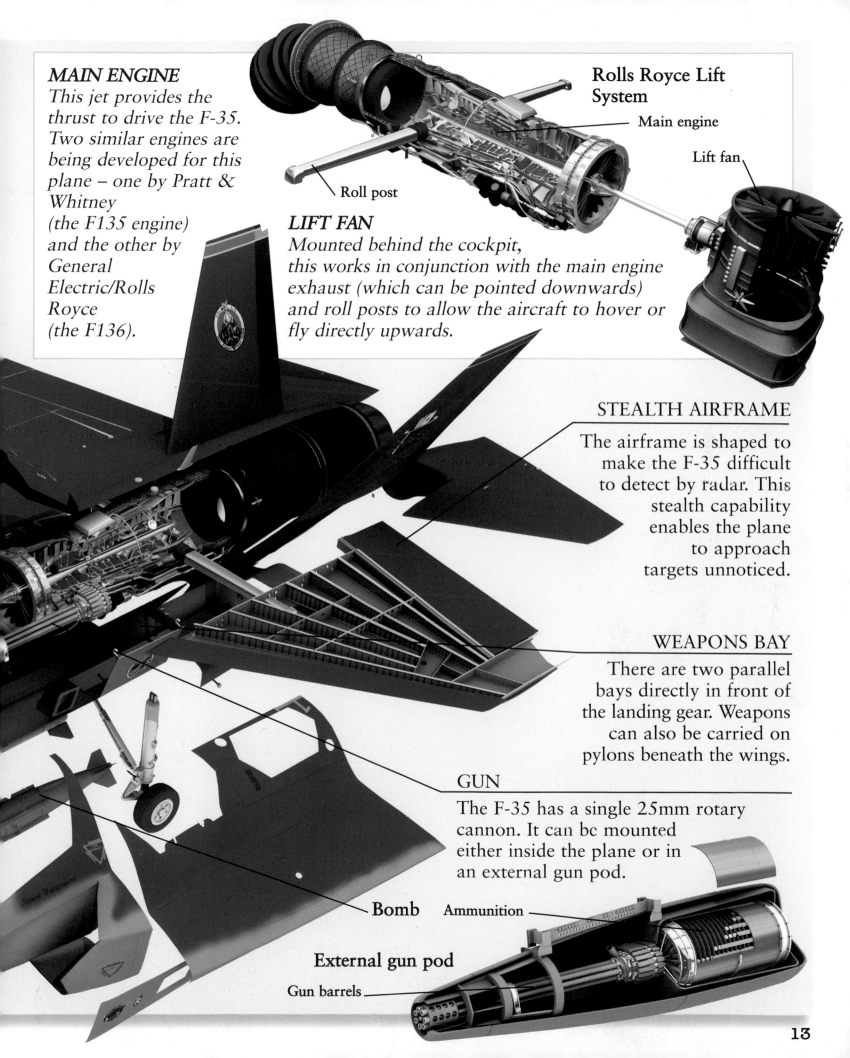

MAIN ENGINE

This jet provides the thrust to drive the F-35. Two similar engines are being developed for this plane – one by Pratt & Whitney (the F135 engine) and the other by General Electric/Rolls Royce (the F136).

Rolls Royce Lift System

Main engine

Lift fan

Roll post

LIFT FAN

Mounted behind the cockpit, this works in conjunction with the main engine exhaust (which can be pointed downwards) and roll posts to allow the aircraft to hover or fly directly upwards.

STEALTH AIRFRAME

The airframe is shaped to make the F-35 difficult to detect by radar. This stealth capability enables the plane to approach targets unnoticed.

WEAPONS BAY

There are two parallel bays directly in front of the landing gear. Weapons can also be carried on pylons beneath the wings.

GUN

The F-35 has a single 25mm rotary cannon. It can be mounted either inside the plane or in an external gun pod.

Bomb

Ammunition

External gun pod

Gun barrels

E-3 SENTRY AWACS

The Boeing E-3 Sentry was produced from 1976 until 1992 and is still in use today. In all, 68 were built for the US, UK, French, Saudi Arabian and NATO air defence forces. The E-3 Sentry is a flying surveillance centre, used mainly for the detection of low-flying aircraft. The letters AWACS stand for Airborne Warning and Control System.

E-3 SENTRY AWACS

Wingspan: 44.4 metres
Length: 46.6 metres
Height: 12.6 metres
Top speed: 855 kilometres per hour

FLIGHT DECK

The four flight crew include a pilot and co-pilot, who fly the aircraft from the deck. The E-3 is a modified Boeing 707 and has similar controls.

Radar

WORKSTATIONS

The E-3 Sentry carries between 13 and 19 mission crew, each with their own workstation. They carry out surveillance, analysing data from the radar antenna system which detects both air and sea targets.

Crew at console

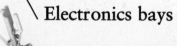
Electronics bays

Undercarriage

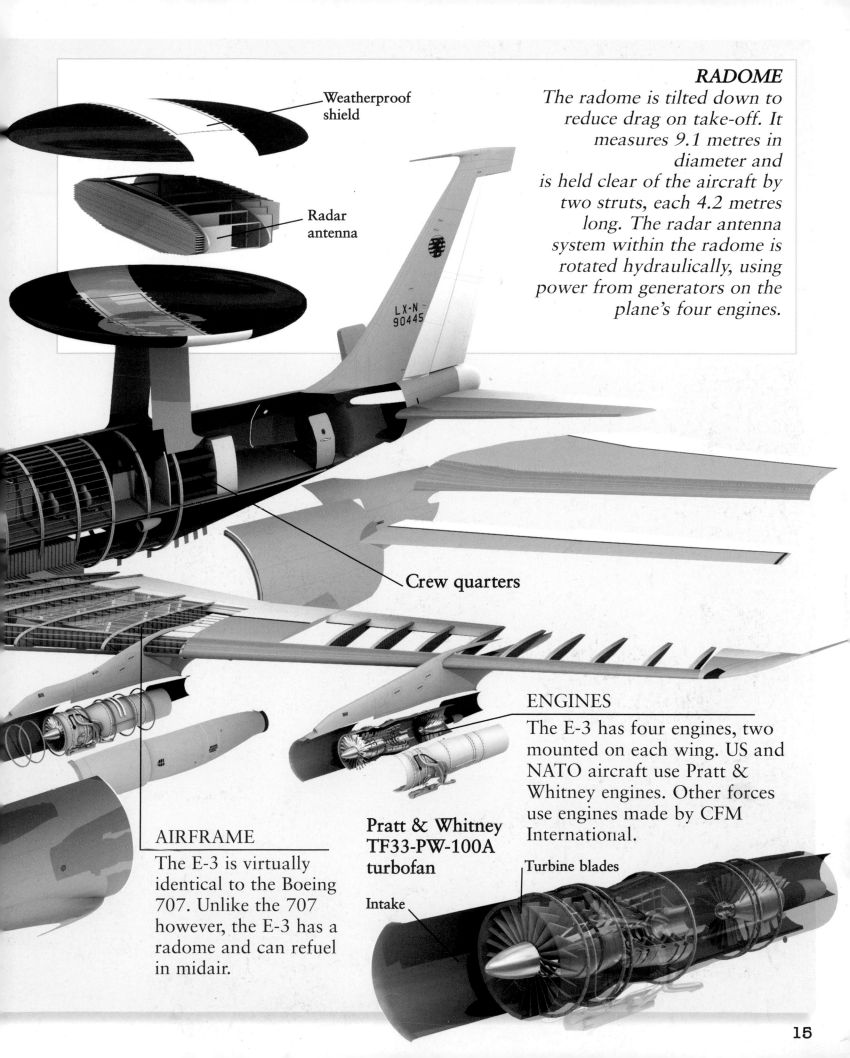

Weatherproof
shield

Radar
antenna

RADOME
The radome is tilted down to reduce drag on take-off. It measures 9.1 metres in diameter and is held clear of the aircraft by two struts, each 4.2 metres long. The radar antenna system within the radome is rotated hydraulically, using power from generators on the plane's four engines.

LX-N
90445

Crew quarters

ENGINES
The E-3 has four engines, two mounted on each wing. US and NATO aircraft use Pratt & Whitney engines. Other forces use engines made by CFM International.

Pratt & Whitney TF33-PW-100A turbofan

AIRFRAME
The E-3 is virtually identical to the Boeing 707. Unlike the 707 however, the E-3 has a radome and can refuel in midair.

Turbine blades

Intake

15

F/A-22 RAPTOR

This state-of-the-art fighter was commissioned for exclusive use by the US Air Force. It is built by the company Lockheed Martin, which began production in 2003. The F/A-22 Raptor is a capable but expensive aircraft – each one costs more than US$175 million.

F/A-22 RAPTOR

Wingspan: 13.6 metres
Length: 18.9 metres
Height: 5.1 metres
Top speed: 2,410 kilometres per hour
Max weapons load: 6,800 kilograms

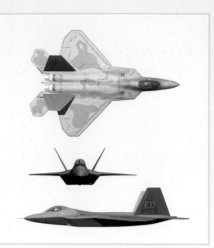

COCKPIT

The cockpit is unusually roomy. The canopy is made from one piece of glass and the ejection seat has a built-in, fast-acting parachute.

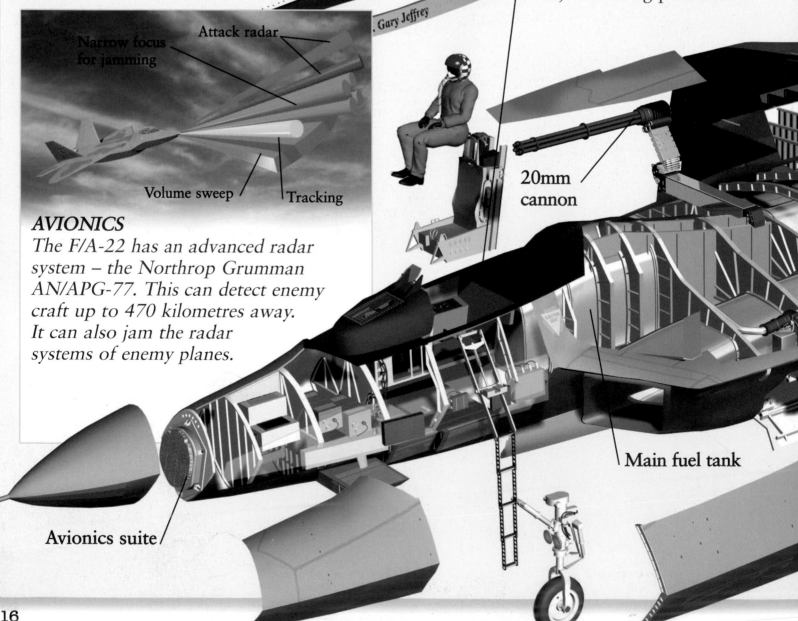

Gary Jeffrey

Narrow focus for jamming

Attack radar

Volume sweep

Tracking

AVIONICS

The F/A-22 has an advanced radar system – the Northrop Grumman AN/APG-77. This can detect enemy craft up to 470 kilometres away. It can also jam the radar systems of enemy planes.

20mm cannon

Main fuel tank

Avionics suite

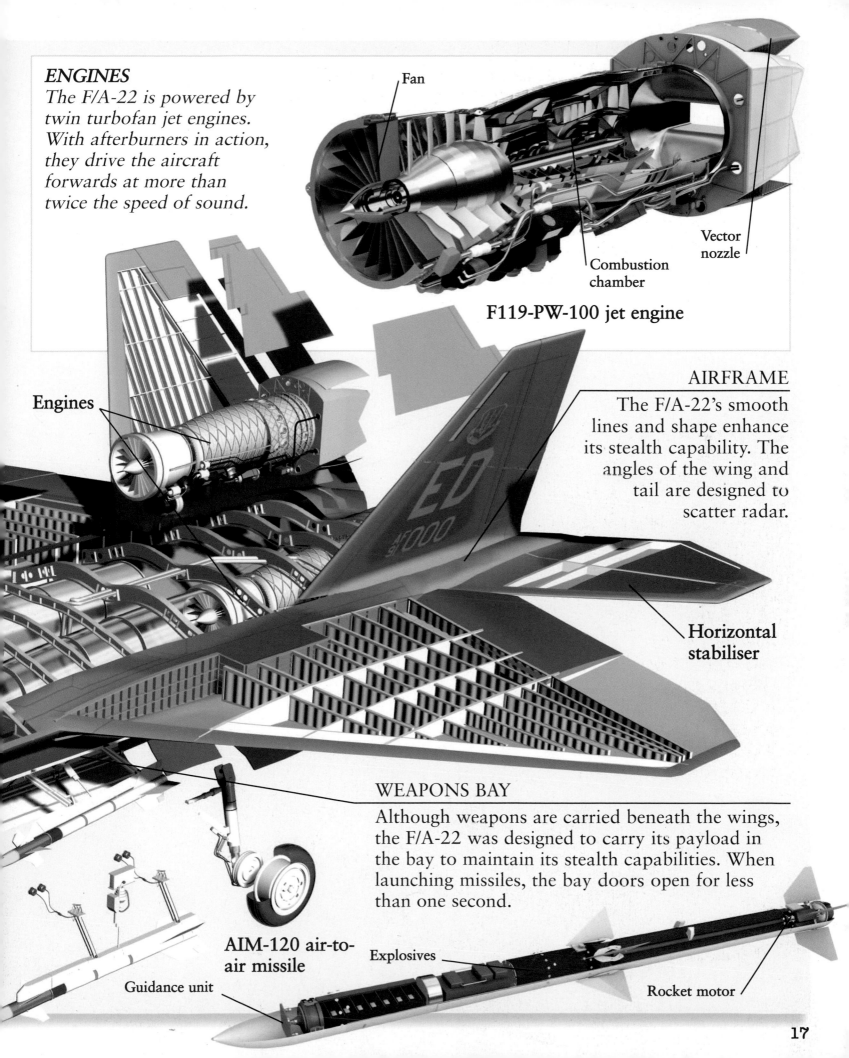

ENGINES

The F/A-22 is powered by twin turbofan jet engines. With afterburners in action, they drive the aircraft forwards at more than twice the speed of sound.

Fan

Vector nozzle

Combustion chamber

F119-PW-100 jet engine

Engines

AIRFRAME

The F/A-22's smooth lines and shape enhance its stealth capability. The angles of the wing and tail are designed to scatter radar.

Horizontal stabiliser

WEAPONS BAY

Although weapons are carried beneath the wings, the F/A-22 was designed to carry its payload in the bay to maintain its stealth capabilities. When launching missiles, the bay doors open for less than one second.

AIM-120 air-to-air missile

Explosives

Guidance unit

Rocket motor

B-2 SPIRIT STEALTH BOMBER

The Cold War prompted the US Air Force to commission the design of the B-2 Spirit Stealth Bomber, but the Soviet Union fell apart before it was completed. A total of 21 B-2s were built and have seen action in Kosovo, Afghanistan and Iraq. The B-2 heavy bomber was designed to carry conventional and nuclear bombs.

STEALTH

The B-2's smooth surface makes it difficult to detect with radar equipment. Its stealth paint absorbs radar.

FLIGHT DECK

The B-2 has a crew of two. The pilot sits in the left seat and the mission commander in the right. The B-2 is highly automated, allowing one crew member to sleep during long missions.

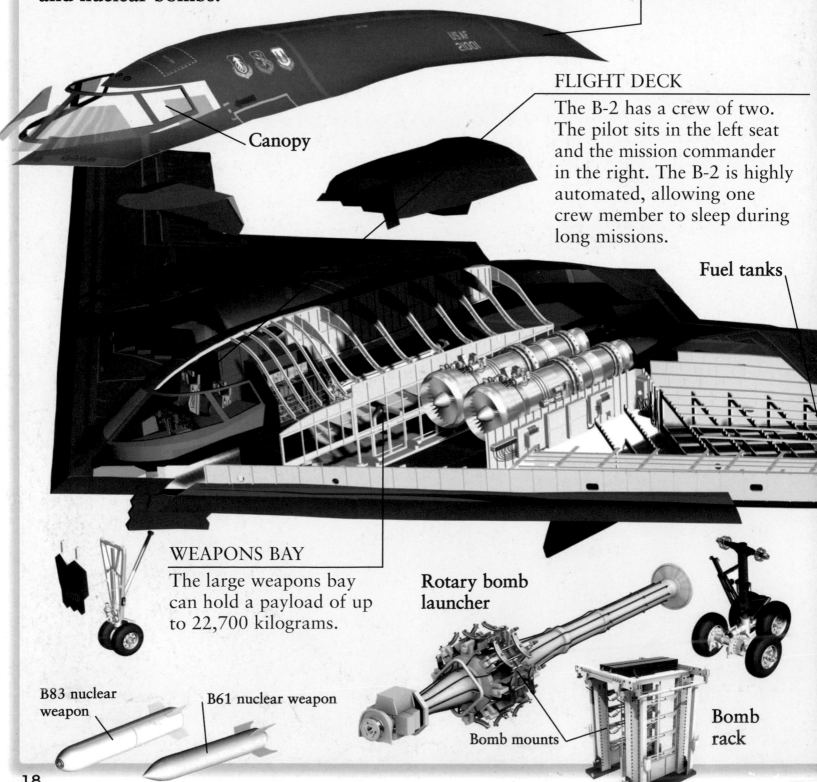

Canopy

Fuel tanks

WEAPONS BAY

The large weapons bay can hold a payload of up to 22,700 kilograms.

Rotary bomb launcher

B83 nuclear weapon

B61 nuclear weapon

Bomb mounts

Bomb rack

F118-GE-100 turbofan engine

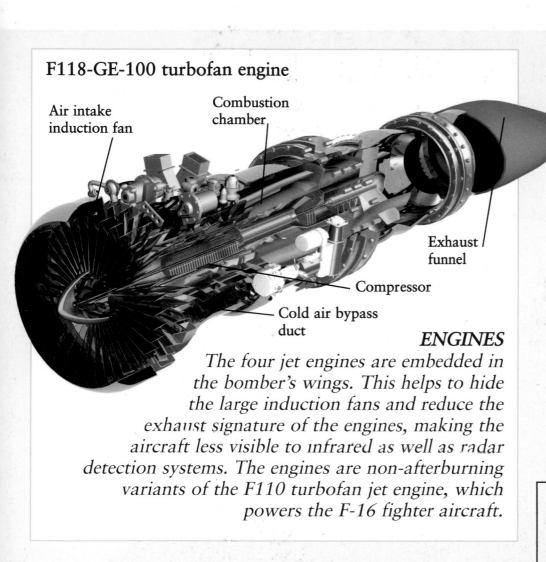

Air intake induction fan

Combustion chamber

Exhaust funnel

Compressor

Cold air bypass duct

NORTHROP GRUMMAN B-2 SPIRIT

Wingspan: 52.4 metres
Length: 21 metres
Height: 5.2 metres
Top speed: 972 kilometres per hour
Max weapons load: 22,700 kilograms

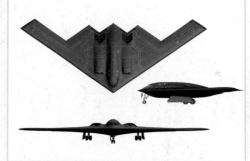

ENGINES

The four jet engines are embedded in the bomber's wings. This helps to hide the large induction fans and reduce the exhaust signature of the engines, making the aircraft less visible to infrared as well as radar detection systems. The engines are non-afterburning variants of the F110 turbofan jet engine, which powers the F-16 fighter aircraft.

AIRFRAME

The B-2's 'flying wing' design reduces the number of leading edges to improve its stealth. The materials in the fuselage are top secret. Computer controlled flying systems make it more stable.

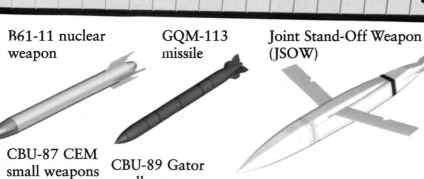

B61-11 nuclear weapon

GQM-113 missile

Joint Stand-Off Weapon (JSOW)

CBU-87 CEM small weapons dispenser

CBU-89 Gator small weapons dispenser

GBU-31 2000 pound Joint Direct Attack Munition (JDAM)

Mk 84 2000-pound bomb

PAYLOAD

The B-2 is designed to carry a wide variety of bombs, including up to 16 B61 or B83 nuclear weapons. During the Kosovo conflict in 1999 it became the first aircraft to carry and deploy GPS satellite guided JDAM 'Smart Bombs'.

A-10 THUNDERBOLT

First made in the 1970s, the A-10 was designed to aid ground troops and crush enemy tanks. The A-10 is not as fast as other jets, but is one of the world's deadliest ground attack aircraft. Known as 'Tankbuster', it can carry a huge weapons load. The armoured cockpit protects the pilot from enemy fire.

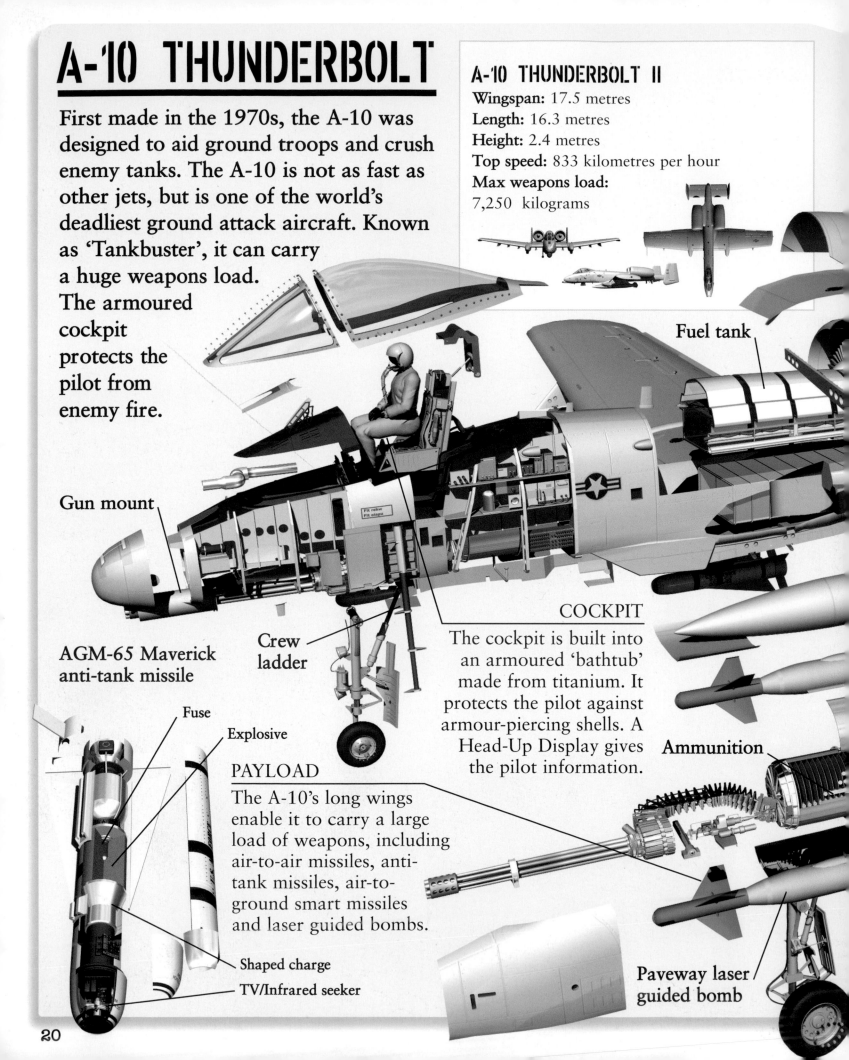

A-10 THUNDERBOLT II

Wingspan: 17.5 metres
Length: 16.3 metres
Height: 2.4 metres
Top speed: 833 kilometres per hour
Max weapons load: 7,250 kilograms

Fuel tank

Gun mount

AGM-65 Maverick anti-tank missile

Crew ladder

Fuse

Explosive

COCKPIT

The cockpit is built into an armoured 'bathtub' made from titanium. It protects the pilot against armour-piercing shells. A Head-Up Display gives the pilot information.

Ammunition

PAYLOAD

The A-10's long wings enable it to carry a large load of weapons, including air-to-air missiles, anti-tank missiles, air-to-ground smart missiles and laser guided bombs.

Shaped charge

TV/Infrared seeker

Paveway laser guided bomb

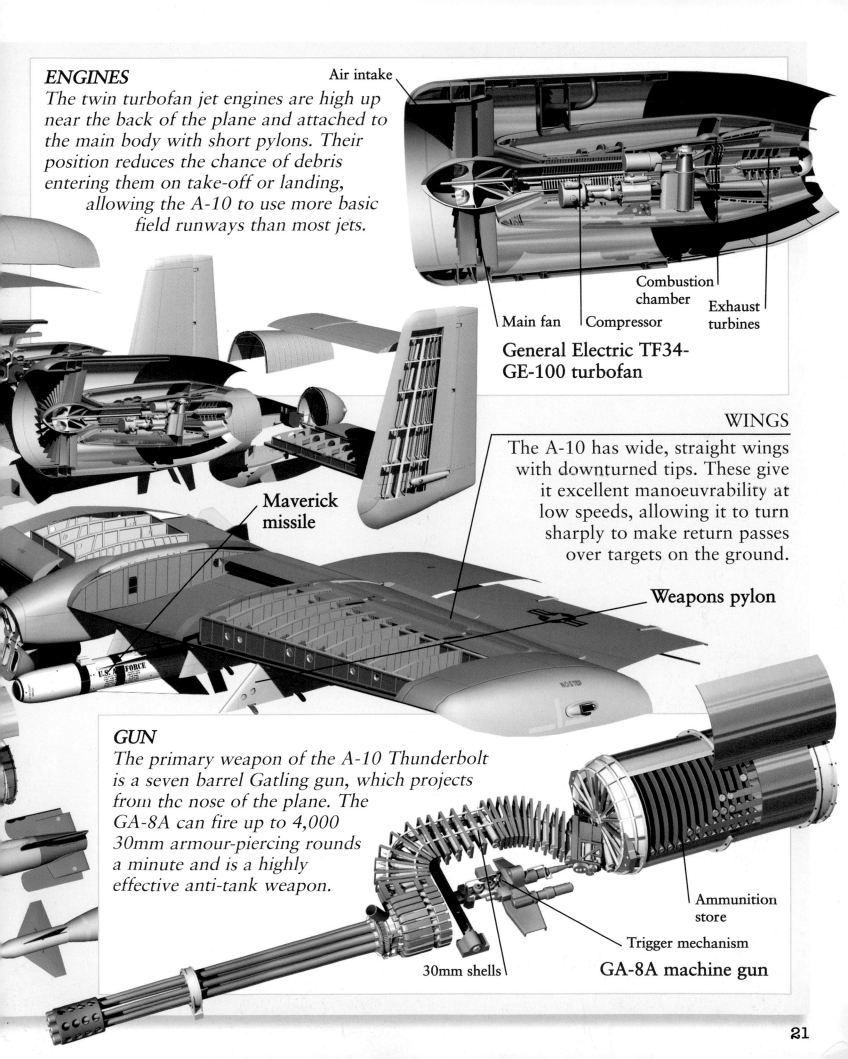

ENGINES

The twin turbofan jet engines are high up near the back of the plane and attached to the main body with short pylons. Their position reduces the chance of debris entering them on take-off or landing, allowing the A-10 to use more basic field runways than most jets.

Air intake

Combustion chamber

Main fan Compressor Exhaust turbines

General Electric TF34-GE-100 turbofan

WINGS

The A-10 has wide, straight wings with downturned tips. These give it excellent manoeuvrability at low speeds, allowing it to turn sharply to make return passes over targets on the ground.

Maverick missile

Weapons pylon

U.S. AIR FORCE

GUN

The primary weapon of the A-10 Thunderbolt is a seven barrel Gatling gun, which projects from the nose of the plane. The GA-8A can fire up to 4,000 30mm armour-piercing rounds a minute and is a highly effective anti-tank weapon.

Ammunition store

Trigger mechanism

30mm shells

GA-8A machine gun

EA-6B PROWLER

The EA-6B Prowler is a specialised plane, designed for locating targets by the electromagnetic radiation (ER) they give off. All devices that contain electronic equipment give off this radiation. The Prowler can pass this information to other planes or attack the targets itself.

EA-6B PROWLER

Wingspan: 15.9 metres
Length: 17.7 metres
Height: 4.9 metres
Top speed: 1,050 kilometres per hour
Max weapons load: 6,810 kilograms

COCKPIT

The cockpit carries four crew members – a pilot and three Electronic Countermeasures Officers (ECMOs). The ECMOs analyse any signals that the Prowler picks up and then convey information to other planes.

CANOPY

The glass within the two-part canopy has a shading of gold to protect the crew from the radio emissions that the Prowler's high-tech equipment gives off.

Ejector seat

Main fuel tank

Mid-air refuelling probe

Nose cone

Fuel drop tank

Engine

NOSE RADAR

This is the main device for detecting ER from enemy targets such as radar stations and surface-to-air missile installations.

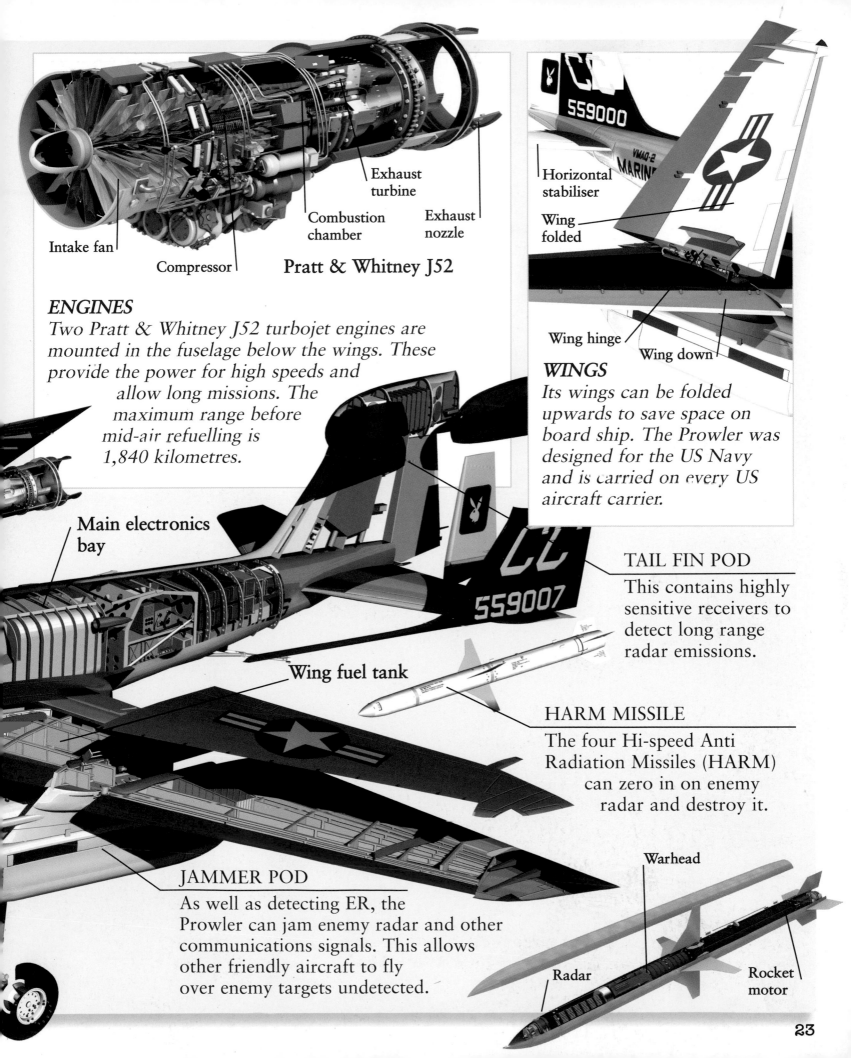

Pratt & Whitney J52

Intake fan

Compressor

Combustion chamber

Exhaust turbine

Exhaust nozzle

ENGINES

Two Pratt & Whitney J52 turbojet engines are mounted in the fuselage below the wings. These provide the power for high speeds and allow long missions. The maximum range before mid-air refuelling is 1,840 kilometres.

Horizontal stabiliser

Wing folded

Wing hinge

Wing down

WINGS

Its wings can be folded upwards to save space on board ship. The Prowler was designed for the US Navy and is carried on every US aircraft carrier.

Main electronics bay

Wing fuel tank

TAIL FIN POD

This contains highly sensitive receivers to detect long range radar emissions.

HARM MISSILE

The four Hi-speed Anti Radiation Missiles (HARM) can zero in on enemy radar and destroy it.

Warhead

JAMMER POD

As well as detecting ER, the Prowler can jam enemy radar and other communications signals. This allows other friendly aircraft to fly over enemy targets undetected.

Radar

Rocket motor

MI-24 HIND MILITARY HELICOPTER

Introduced in 1972, the MI-24 Hind Military Helicopter is an assault gunship developed and built in the Soviet Union. It is still used by Russian forces today and by the air forces of over 30 other nations. The MI-24 has seen active service in numerous conflicts. It is a highly effective gunship that can also act as a troop transporter.

MI-24 HIND MILITARY HELICOPTER

Rotor diameter: 17.3 metres
Length: 17.5 metres
Height: 6.5 metres
Top speed: 335 kilometres per hour
Max weapons load: 1,480 kilograms

Exhaust port

Engines

ROTOR BLADES

The MI-24 uses a five-blade main rotor driven by two top-mounted engines featuring twin air intakes.

COCKPIT

The cockpit seats two or three crew, with the gunner in front of the pilot. It is armoured to withstand direct hits from 20mm rounds.

Yak-B 12.7mm machine gun

Swivel mount

12.7MM GUN TURRET

The mobile turret beneath the helicopter's nose carries a four-barrel Gatling gun with 1,470 rounds. The gun is controlled remotely from the cockpit.

Retractable undercarriage

Transport compartment

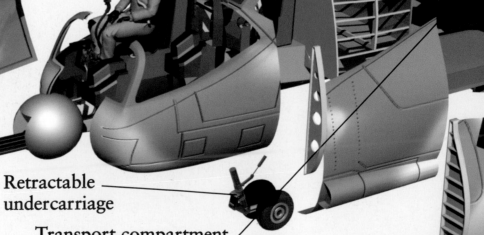

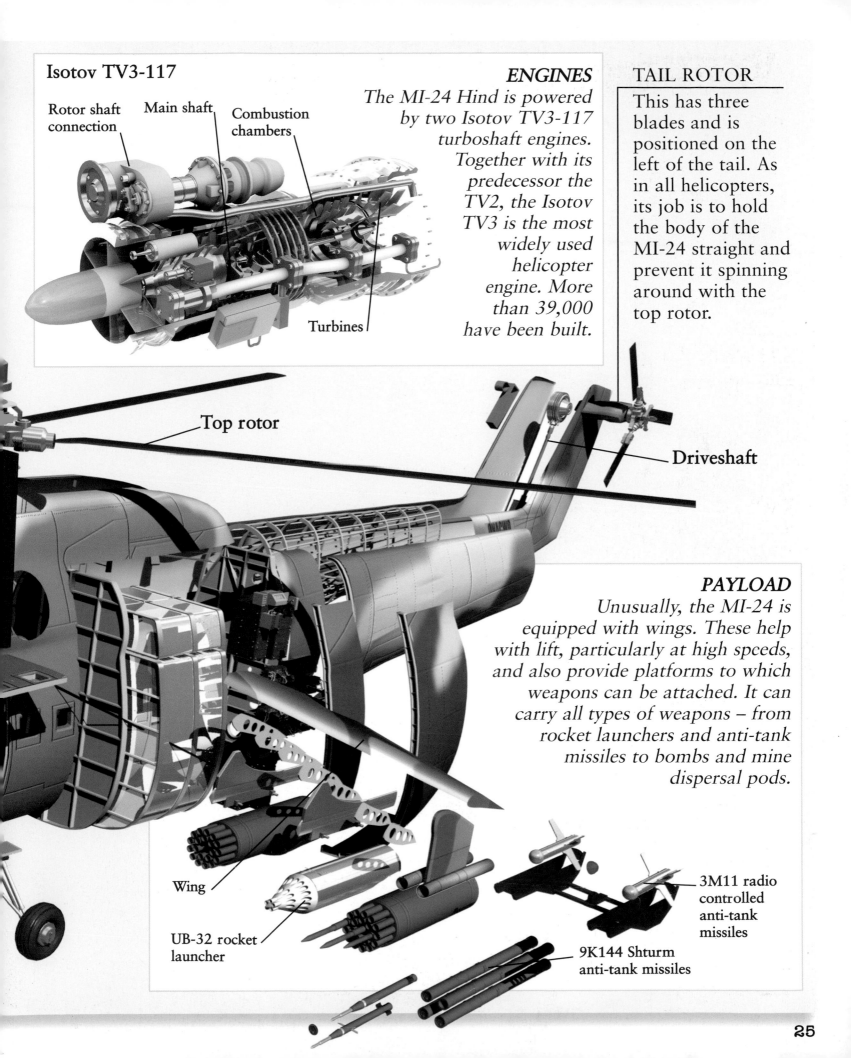

Isotov TV3-117

Rotor shaft connection

Main shaft

Combustion chambers

Turbines

ENGINES

The MI-24 Hind is powered by two Isotov TV3-117 turboshaft engines. Together with its predecessor the TV2, the Isotov TV3 is the most widely used helicopter engine. More than 39,000 have been built.

TAIL ROTOR

This has three blades and is positioned on the left of the tail. As in all helicopters, its job is to hold the body of the MI-24 straight and prevent it spinning around with the top rotor.

Top rotor

Driveshaft

PAYLOAD

Unusually, the MI-24 is equipped with wings. These help with lift, particularly at high speeds, and also provide platforms to which weapons can be attached. It can carry all types of weapons – from rocket launchers and anti-tank missiles to bombs and mine dispersal pods.

Wing

UB-32 rocket launcher

3M11 radio controlled anti-tank missiles

9K144 Shturm anti-tank missiles

AC-130 SPOOKY GUNSHIP

The AC-130 is a heavily-armed ground attack gunship based on the C-130 Hercules transport plane. Used exclusively by the US Air Force, it supports ground troops by firing on hostile forces, and can escort convoys of trucks and other vehicles through dangerous territory.

AC-130 SPECTRE/SPOOKY

Wingspan: 40.4 metres

Length: 29.8 metres

Height: 11.7 metres

Top speed: 480 kilometres per hour

Max weapons load: 10,170 kilograms

Ammunition store

Flight deck

Navigation radar and moving target indicator

FIRE CONTROL

The Spooky uses complex targeting technology, including video, infrared and radar sensors. Firing of the weapons is controlled from this unit in the plane's centre.

25MM ROTARY CANNON

The five-barrel Gatling gun can fire up to 1,800 rounds per minute. All of the Spooky's weapons project from the left side of the plane.

Night vision radar

Ammunition feed

Gun barrel

GAU-12/U Equaliser Gatling gun

AIRFRAME

The airframe of the AC-130 is identical to that of the C-130 Hercules, which has been in production for over 50 years. Each wing contains two fuel tanks – one for each of the engines suspended underneath.

Loading bay

UF 8668

ENGINES

The four Allison T56-A-15 turboprop engines give the AC-130 a mission range of 4,070 kilometres.

Howitzer

Bofors gun

FIREPOWER

The AC-130 has three types of weapon for a range of targets. The Gatling gun and Bofors gun are used against lightly-armoured ground targets. The howitzer, which can fire 10 rounds a minute, is used against tanks and fortified gun emplacements. If necessary, two different weapons can be fired at once.

Barrel rest

105mm howitzer

40mm Bofors gun

Recoil spring

Size of 105mm shell

V-22 OSPREY

The V-22 Osprey began service with the US Marine Corps and Air Force in 2005. It combines the long range and superior speed of a turboprop aircraft with the vertical take-off capability of a helicopter.

V-22 using load hooks in flight

LOAD BAY

Used for carrying troops or supplies, the rear door can open in flight to allow troops to parachute out. The V-22 is equipped with hooks for carrying loads underneath.

Rotor forward flight

ROTORS

At take-off, the massive rotors are tilted upwards. Once airborne, it takes only 12 seconds to rotate the rotors forwards for horizontal flight.

Canopy

COCKPIT

The large glass canopy in the cockpit offers excellent visibility. Four Multi-Function Display screens with a Central Display Unit show images such as maps and infrared views of the land ahead.

Multi-Function Display screen

Central Display Unit

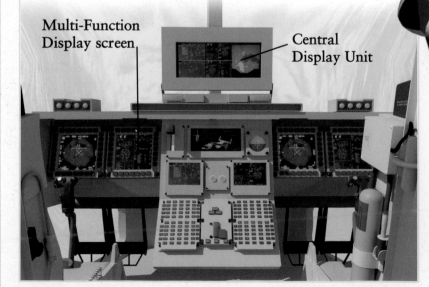

Wings folded

Props folded

V-22 storage position

V-22 OSPREY

Rotor diameter: 11.6 metres
Length: 17.5 metres
Height: 6.7 metres
Top speed: 565 kilometres per hour
Max weapons load: N/A

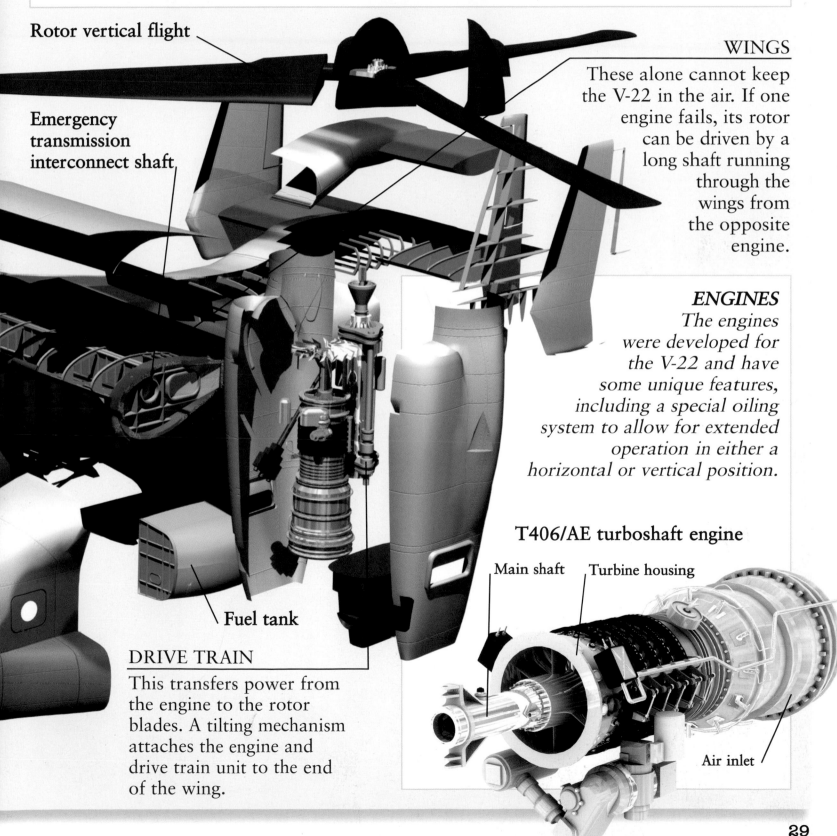

Rotor vertical flight

Emergency transmission interconnect shaft

Fuel tank

WINGS
These alone cannot keep the V-22 in the air. If one engine fails, its rotor can be driven by a long shaft running through the wings from the opposite engine.

ENGINES
The engines were developed for the V-22 and have some unique features, including a special oiling system to allow for extended operation in either a horizontal or vertical position.

T406/AE turboshaft engine

Main shaft   Turbine housing

Air inlet

DRIVE TRAIN
This transfers power from the engine to the rotor blades. A tilting mechanism attaches the engine and drive train unit to the end of the wing.

FUTURE MACHINES

Even as the latest military aircraft enter service, new ones are being developed to replace them. The threat of enemy success means military aircraft design and technology is constantly progressing, aiming to achieve the best performance.

EA-18G GROWLER
This plane will soon enter service with the US Navy. It will escort and 'hide' fighter planes by jamming enemy radar systems.

Modern military aircraft include some of the fastest, most advanced and most expensive vehicles in the world. Each one is designed and tested over several years before it enters service. These planes show the variety of what we might see in the future.

PREDATOR
Designed for reconnaissance at medium altitude, this small plane is unmanned.

GLOBAL HAWK
Like the Predator, the Global Hawk is remotely controlled and used for surveillance. It is much bigger however, and flies at higher altitudes to survey larger areas.

X-45 UCAV
Another unmanned and remotely controlled plane, the X-45, is being developed to undertake bombing missions.

GLOSSARY

afterburner
A component of some jet engines used to provide a sudden boost in thrust.

airframe
The basic structure of an aircraft.

biplane
A plane with two sets of main wings, one directly above the other.

ejection seat
A seat designed to eject the pilot from the cockpit in an emergency.

electromagnetic radiation
Radiation or waves emitted by objects, including radio and radar, microwaves, infrared light, visible light and X-rays.

electro-optical targeting
Targeting using electromagnetic radiation signals other than those in the optical (visible) spectrum, i.e. other than light.

fuselage
The central body of an aircraft, to which the wings and tail are attached.

head-up display
An electronically generated display of data superimposed on the inside of the cockpit canopy or the inside of the pilot's visor.

infrared
Electromagnetic radiation just beyond the red end of the light spectrum.

non-orthogonal
Not containing right angles.

radar
Ra(dio) d(etection) a(nd) r(anging). A method of detecting objects using very high frequency radio waves.

stealth technology
Aspects of an aircraft's design that help it avoid detection by radar or other means.

supersonic
Faster than the speed of sound – 1,235 kilometres per hour.

tiltrotor
An engine and rotor blade assembly that can be tilted from vertical to horizontal.

turbofan engine
A jet engine with a large front fan (intake turbine) that forces air into the engine and also blows air around the engine for extra thrust.

turboprop engine
A turboshaft engine with a gear system to turn a propeller.

turboshaft engine
A jet engine whose central shaft drives another shaft instead of a propellor or fan.

undercarriage
The wheels and landing gear of an aircraft.

INDEX